D1173641
DINGLE
CHAM

LIGHTS OUT™

Lights Out Vol. 1

Created by Myung-Jin Lee

Translation - Ellen Choi
English Adaptation - Jess Stoncius
Copy Editor - Hope Donovan
Retouch and Lettering - James Lee
Production Artist - Gloria Wu and Jason Milligan
Cover Design - Gary Shum

Editor - Tim Beedle
Digital Imaging Manager - Chris Buford
Production Managers - Jennifer Miller and Mutsumi Miyazaki
Managing Editor - Lindsey Johnston
VP of Production - Ron Klamert
Publisher and E.I.C. - Mike Kiley
President and C.O.O. - John Parker
C.E.O. - Stuart Levy

A  Manga

TOKYOPOP Inc.
5900 Wilshire Blvd. Suite 2000
Los Angeles, CA 90036

E-mail: info@TOKYOPOP.com
Come visit us online at www.TOKYOPOP.com

ISBN: 1-59532-360-0

First TOKYOPOP printing: October 2005

10 9 8 7 6 5 4 3 2 1

Printed in the USA

TOKYOPOP®

HAMBURG // LONDON // LOS ANGELES // TOKYO

LIGHTS OUT™

VOLUME 1 :: MYUNG-JIN LEE

A Short Word
DIVE TO DREAM SEA
Hi! This is Myung-Jin Lee.

This is my debut work, *Lights Out.* (Just so you know, the original title is *An Evening Something Wonderful May Happen.*)

After ten years, we're putting it in the spotlight again. Like presenting a face without any makeup, I would like to present to you *Lights Out* just as it was 10 years ago...warts and all. Kind of embarrassing, but I hope you enjoy it.

Myung-Jin Lee
April, 2002

LIGHTS OUT™
남궁 건 등장
챔프
어쩐지 좋은 일이
HOLLY WOOD JIN
400
STUDIO
GRAFFITY
SECS
IN SEOUL
BY HOLLY WOOD
TUNED BY
Myung-Jin Lee

Next stop is Kang-Byun station. Please exit to your right.
Gung-Gun Nam
17 years old
NEWSPAPER HEADLINE: Frog Boys Make the Majors!
WHAT THE HELL IS THAT?!
Hrmph.
UH, YOU LOOK TIRED, MA'AM. WHY DON'T YOU TAKE MY--
HEE HEE! DON'T MIND IF I DO, WHIPPER-SNAPPER!
THAT OLD BAT WAS AFTER MY SEAT!
The door will open.
UNGH?

Seung-Ah Min
17 years old
DAMN!
SHE'S BEAUTIFUL!
덜컹
덜컹

Next stop is Sung-Soo. Please exit to your right.
Please board in an orderly fashion.
MY SEAT! MY SEAT, BOYO!!
HEY, MAN! STOP WITH THE SHOVING!
EWW! DON'T PUSH ME THERE!
와글와글
CUT IT OUT!
IT'S NICE TO SEE THAT SOME THINGS HAVEN'T CHANGED... LIKE RUSH HOUR.
DAMMIT! STOP PUSHING!
OW!
!!

MAN, THAT WAS TOO CLOSE.
THESE LOSERS ALMOST PUSHED ME RIGHT UP AGAINST HER...
CRAP...
I'M GONNA BE CHEST GROPING HER IF I DON'T DO SOMETHING!
?
UNGH...
UGH...
!!
MUST...NOT... CRUSH...BABE...
KHWWWWAAAAAAAAAAHH!
I CAN'T BREATHE!
CROWDS MAKE ME HURL!
DON'T HURL IN HERE, DUMB-ASS!

덜컹덜컹
Huff! Huff!
MAN, DID YOU SEE HER? I CAN'T BELIEVE HE'S PUSHING HIMSELF AWAY!
YEAH! WHO WOULDN'T WANNA GET CLOSE TO THAT?
COZY THE FOX
NRGH...
I SWEAR I'M GONNA HURL NOW!
I SAID NOT IN HERE, YOU IDIOT!
STOP PUSHING!
Next stop is Dongdaemun station. Please exit to your right...
?!
A STATION? THAT MEANS A LOT OF PEOPLE ARE GONNA GET OFF NOW, RIGHT?
THIS GUY!!
HUH?!

WHAAAT?!
LORD, PLEASE DELIVER ME FROM THE TEMPTATION OF HER FORBIDDEN FRUIT.
Another train will be arriving soon. Please take the next train if possible.
NEXT TRAIN? SCREW THAT!
NO MORE PEOPLE!
NO MORE PUSHING!
HUH?!

NO! AFTER ALL MY HARD WORK!
...TOUCH...
MY CHEST IS GONNA...
DOINK!♥

GAH!
THWAAAK!

MY BODY... IT FEELS LIKE... I'M ALL FLOATY!
TH-THUMP
TH-THUMP
TH-THUMP
TH-THUMP
BA-DUMP
BA-DUMP
WITH HIM SO NEARBY... JUST BY HIS STRONG PRESENCE...
Huff!
BA-DUMP
BA-DUMP
Hah!
Huh!
BA-DUMP
BA-DUMP
I FEEL LIKE I'M BEING SWEPT AWAY!

I THINK I'M GONNA PASS OUT...
NO, I CAN'T GO OUT LIKE THAT!
RAAAHHR!
ACK! HE'S GONNA PUSH AGAIN!
WELL, LET'S JUST PUSH HIM BACK!
LET'S SHOW HIM WHAT WE'RE MADE OF!
...!!
WE SHALL OVERCOME!!
HAYAAA!
GRRRR!!
WHAT'S WITH ALL THE NOISE?
DON'T YOU KNOW NOISE ONLY MAKES IT EASIER FOR ME TO TAKE YOUR MONEY?!

HYAAAAAAAA!!
THAT GUY'S NOT HUMAN!
HE'S LIKE THE HULK!
WE'RE ALL GONNA GET SMASHED!!!

KA-DUM
WHAT'S WRONG WITH ME? I CAN'T HEAR ANYTHING...
KA-DUM
KA-DUM
KA-DUM
KA-DUM
KA-DUM
...EXCEPT THE BEATING OF MY HEART.
WAKE UP, SEUNG-AH! HE'S JUST SOME STRANGER YOU MET ON A CROWDED SUBWAY TRAIN.
KA-DUM
KA-DUM
The pickpocket
수군
OH, I LOVE MY WORK! ABSOLUTELY LOVE IT! I LOVE HOW IT GETS ME MONEY. I LOVE HOW IT GETS ME CLOSE TO PEOPLE. OH, IT'S GREAT TO HAVE A JOB YOU CAN GET EXCITED ABOUT!
와글와글
Next stop is Uljiro station.
SEEMS LIKE A GOOD TIME TO LEAVE...
HUH?
덜컹덜컹
덜컹덜컹

OH MY! SUCH A STRONG BOY! I BET HE HAS A BIG WALLET.
DON'T MOVE...
IT'S SO THICK! NO WONDER HE HAS SUCH LUCK WITH THE LADIES!
EXCUSE ME, DID YOU LOSE YOUR WALLET, BY ANY CHANCE?
HUH?
IT'S NOT THE ONE THAT CREEPY GUY'S HOLDING, IS IT?
OH NO! IT'S GONE! MY RENT! MY TUITION!
So pretty!
STUDIO GRAFFITY
HEY!!
GIMME BACK MY WALLET, YOU CREEP!!
OOPSIE!
STUDIO GRAFFITY
콰르릉

WELL, I SEEM TO HAVE WORN OUT MY WELCOME. IT'S TIME TO SPLIT!
ARGH!
STOP RIGHT THERE, YOU JERK!!
SILLY BOY! DO YOU REALLY THINK I'M GONNA STOP JUST BECAUSE YOU TELL ME TO?
YOU CAN RUN, BUT YOU CAN'T HIDE!
Neebok
GRAFFITY
The train will soon be departing. All aboard!
THANK GOD THAT GUY IS GONE!
HE'S GONE...
BUT...
...WHAT'S THIS FEELING IN MY HEART?
COULD IT BE...?
Next stop is Shi-Chung... Eh?
What's this fly doing here?

STOP, YOU ASSHOLE!!
UL-JINO
?!!
AND THE DAY WAS GOING SO SMOOTHLY UNTIL NOW... I GUESS HE REALLY WANTS HIS MONEY BACK.
ROASTED NUTS FOR SALE!
YAAAH!
I NEED TO BORROW THIS!
HA HA HA! I'LL SEE YOU IN HELL!
GOODBYE! MWAH HA HA!!
AH, NUTS!!

THWAK!!
HIYA!!
KABOOM!
을지로 입구
ULJINO-2ga
2
Neebok
WOW! JUST LIKE IN THE VIDEO GAMES!
CLENCH!
YOU'RE NOT GONNA GET AWAY, SO GIVE IT BACK RIGHT NOW!
GEE, I GUESS YOU WIN...

...NOT!

YOU THINK I'M CRAZY?!

COME BACK HERE!

GET AWAY!

ACK!!

SIGN: Monsieur Nikolai 2nd Flr.

I-I... I LOST HIM!

ARRGH!! MY RENT! MY TUITION! I'LL BE HOMELESS AND UNEDUCATED FOREVER!

HEH...

My life was in that wallet! Give it back! Waaaah!

HEH...

IS DIS DA BRAT YOU WAS TALKIN' ABOUT?
YES! LEAVING THAT GUY FREE TO ROAM THE STREETS IS ONLY GOING TO CAUSE MORE GRIEF FOR ALL THE HARDWORKING PICKPOCKETS OUT THERE. SHOW 'EM WHO'S BOSS, BOSS!

OW!
?!
WHAT'RE YOU LOOKIN' AT? ARE YOU LOOKIN' AT ME?
DAMN, HE'S REALLY BIG! AND THAT TIE IS REALLY UGLY!

HEH HEH! N-NO, I WAS JUST THINKING ABOUT SOMETHING ELSE. I'M SORRY.

ViLLA

HEY!
You're so dead.
YOU DAMN PICKPOCKET!!
Heh heh...
HOLD ON.

D'YOU REALLY THINK SORRY'S GONNA CUT IT?

IT'S A TRICK...

WELL, IF I REMEMBER CORRECTLY, YOU BUMPED INTO ME... SO IT'S NOT TOTALLY MY FAULT.
FASION
ViLL
Ha ha ha!

↑That's the pickpocket.

YOU MESSIN' WIT ME, KID?!
THWOG!
FIGHT!
SOME FIGHT. THE LITTLE GUY'S NOT EVEN FIGHTING BACK...
ALL RIGHT! A FIGHT! THIS IS LIKE GETTING PAY-PER-VIEW FOR FREE!
HMM? WAIT...
IS THAT WHO I THINK IT IS?!
Na-Rae Shin
17 years old

LIGHTS OUT™

IS THAT GUNG-GUN? FROM JI-JON HIGH? OMIGOD, IT **IS** GUN!!

HIS VICTORIES ARE LEGENDARY! ONE BY ONE, HE'S MANAGED TO DEFEAT THE BEST FIGHTERS FROM EVERY SCHOOL IN THE AREA!

I'D SAY DIS IS YER UNLUCKY DAY!
THWAAK!!

HEH... UH, MAYBE I *DID* BUMP INTO YOU, NOW THAT I THINK ABOUT IT. SORRY ABOUT THAT.
Ha ha ha!

NO, IT CAN'T BE HIM. GUN WOULD NEVER HUMILIATE HIMSELF LIKE THIS.

LOOKS LIKE YOU STILL GOT THE STRENGTH TO TALK. WELL, LET'S JUS' SEE HOW MUCH YOU TALK WHEN I...

...BREAK YER DAMN JAW!!

WOW! THAT REALLY HURT...

Heh heh...

LOOK, I'M REALLY SORRY FOR BUMPING INTO YOU.

WHAT DA HELL KINDA PUNK IS DIS POLITE?!

SHUT YER HOLE!

OH NO!!!

I SAID I WAS SORRY. REALLY, REALLY SORRY...
WELL, HE'S GOT STAMINA. I GUESS IT COULD BE HIM...
Is your neck SUPPOSED to bend like that?
DUDE! HIS HEAD'S BLEEDING!
BLOOD...

DAT SCRATCH IS GONNA BE GUSHING IN A MINUTE!!
YAAAAAAAAH!
WOOOOOHAAAAA!!!

HAH!!!

EGH!!

OOPS! I PROBABLY SHOULD HAVE BEEN MORE PATIENT...
Heh heh...
Ha ha!

THAT HAS TO BE HIM! I'VE SEEN HIM FROM A DISTANCE A COUPLE TIMES, BUT NEVER THIS CLOSE. THOSE SKILLS... NO WONDER HE'S A LEGEND! BUT WHY DID HE LET THAT GUY KNOCK HIM AROUND FOR SO LONG?

HEY!
Sir...
FC

HERE'S YOUR WALLET BACK! BYE!
...!

EXCUSE ME, BUT DO YOU KNOW WHO OWNS THAT SHOP?
HUH? OH, UH... BY THE DOOR.

MOMMY!
FASION VILLAG

UH...ARE YOU THE OWNER OF THIS SHOP?
YES. YES, I AM.

SO...THAT'S A STORE WINDOW AND THREE BROKEN MANNEQUINS, PLUS MONEY FOR CLEANING THE BLOOD OFF THE SIDEWALK AND REMOVING TEETH FROM THE WALL... THE TOTAL DAMAGE COMES TO...
...!
GUESS
FASION
VALLAGE

HA! NOW I HAVE SOMETHING TO BRAG ABOUT TO SEUNG-AH TOMORROW! THE LEGENDARY GUNG-GUN NAM ACTUALLY TALKED TO ME!
captain
토독

DAMN... SO I GUESS I'M OUT OF MONEY FOR THIS MONTH.

I GOT MY WALLET BACK, BUT I'M *STILL* OUT TUITION MONEY AND TWO MONTHS' RENT.
PULL

HMM... SO... 717-7777... LUCKY RESIDENCE...

UMM... ACTUALLY, I'M SUPPOSED TO BE RENTING A ROOM THERE STARTING TODAY. RIGHT NOW, I'M AT MYUNG-DONG VILLAGE, AND I WAS WONDERING IF YOU COULD GIVE ME DIRECTIONS...
SURE, NO PROBLEM. FROM THERE, YOU NEED TO GET ON THE SUBWAY, GET OFF AT DONGDAEMUN STATION AND...

HELLO, THIS IS LUCKY RESIDENCE.
두군
OH MAN, WHAT A SEXY VOICE...

ALL RIGHT!! LET'S GO!!

MY NAME IS GUNG-GUN NAM, BUT EVERYONE JUST CALLS ME GUN. I'M THE NEW TENANT IN THE LUCKY RESIDENCE DORMITORY. ALTHOUGH I JUST GOT INTO A SCRAPE, I CAN'T HELP BUT FEEL THAT SOMETHING WONDERFUL MIGHT HAPPEN TODAY!
WOOHOO!
TO BE WITH YOU

HOLLY WOOD JIN
GRANDPA, YOU HAD A PHONE CALL.
EH?
RASING
TELL HIM TO COME BACK LATER! I AIN'T FIXED HIS CARBURETOR YET.
NO! IT'S THE NEW TENANT. YOU KNOW, THE ONE THAT'S MOVING IN TODAY.
REALLY? THEN CAN YOU CLEAN UP HIS ROOM FOR HIM?
번쩍
SURE, GRANDPA!
MY NAME IS SEUNG-AH. EVER SINCE MY PARENTS PASSED AWAY, I'VE BEEN MANAGING THE LUCKY RESIDENCE WITH MY GRANDFATHER, WHO ALSO RUNS A MOTORCYCLE REPAIR SHOP.
RESIDENTS COME AND GO ALL THE TIME, BUT I KEEP GETTING THE NAGGING FEELING THAT SOMETHING WONDERFUL MAY HAPPEN TODAY.
HOLLY WOOD JIN
The girl from the subway?!

HEH!
HEH!

IT'S GOTTA BE AROUND HERE! I DIDN'T MAKE A WRONG TURN AGAIN, DID I?

HUH?

Gun gets lost easily.

THAT'S THE PLACE RIGHT THERE!

OH MAN, IT'S PAST MIDNIGHT. I CAN'T WAKE EVERYBODY UP THIS LATE!

A LIGHT! SOMEBODY'S UP! MAYBE THIS *IS* A LUCKY RESIDENCE...

BUT WHO'D BE UP AT THIS HOUR? MAYBE THE GIRL WHO GAVE ME DIRECTIONS...?

Heh...

SHE STAYED UP THIS LATE JUST FOR ME! WELL, I'D BETTER NOT KEEP HER WAITING!

I'VE BEEN WAITING ALL NIGHT JUST FOR YOU, BIG BOY.

Gun's fantasy gal

Heh heh...

HEY, YOU! WHAT'RE YOU LOOKIN' IN MY WINDOW FOR THIS LATE AT NIGHT? WERE YA HOPIN' FOR A FREE SHOW?!

NAH, I KNOW WHAT'S GOIN' ON. YOU JUST WANT A LOOK AT MY SEUNG-AH. WELL, SHE'S ALREADY IN BED, SO YOU CAN JUST GO HOME.

EH, NO, THAT'S NOT IT... MY NAME'S GUN. I'M RENTING A ROOM HERE.
SEUNG-AH? IS THAT HER? WHAT A PRETTY NAME.

YOU ARE?
YEP!
?

GETTIN' HERE A BIT LATE, AREN'T YA? FOLLOW ME.
UH...YES, SIR!

AND OH YEAH, LOOK OUT FOR THAT THIRD FLOORBOARD. IT'S KINDA FUNNY.
YOW!

SEUNG-AH, COME IN HERE A SEC! WE HAVE A GUEST.
THE OLD MAN'S GOT LOUSY TIMING.

A GUEST? NOW? GRANDPA?
AGH!

NGH!
THAT'S SO SWEET!
GRANDPA!

I'M FINE. LEMME INTRODUCE YOU TWO. SEUNG-AH, THIS IS OUR NEW RESIDENT, GUN.

GUN, THIS IS MY GRANDDAUGHTER, SEUNG-AH. I THINK YOU TWO ARE THE SAME AGE.

BOIING!!

IT'S THE GIRL FROM THE SUBWAY!
DOINK!♥
KWOK!
IT'S THE GUY FROM THE SUBWAY!
I NEED TO LIE DOWN. SEUNG-AH, SHOW HIM HIS ROOM. **HIS** ROOM! NOT ***YOURS!*** CRAZY KIDS... ALWAYS WITH THE PIERCING AND THE SHACKING UP...
HUH? OH, OKAY!
......
Awkward silence! Yes!
N-NICE TO MEET YOU. I'M GUNG-GUN NAM. BUT CALL ME GUN.
Ha ha ha!
하하하
I'M SEUNG-AH. NICE TO MEET YOU, TOO.
......

UH...YOU MUST BE REALLY TIRED. I'LL SHOW YOU TO YOUR ROOM. JUST FOLLOW ME.
SURE!

IT'S ON THE SECOND FLOOR?!

HUH? OH YEAH, THAT SOUNDS GREAT. BUT THIS IS ONLY A TWO-STORY BUILDING? DON'T YOU HAVE A THIRD FLOOR?

2F

THERE'S A ROOM THAT I USED TO SLEEP IN WHEN I WAS A LITTLE GIRL. YOU CAN USE THAT ROOM.

HA HA! I'M SO GLAD TO BE ALIVE! THANK YOU, GOD!

THIS WAY, PLEASE.
HA HA! LUCKY RESIDENCE... THAT'S FOR DAMN SURE. IF SHE'S THE OWNER HERE, I MUSTA DIED AND GONE TO HEAVEN!

IT'S THE LAST ROOM ON THE RIGHT, AND THE BATHROOM IS RIGHT NEXT TO THE STAIRCASE.
W.C

IT'S REALLY LATE, SO HAVE A GOOD NIGHT.
YEAH, G'NIGHT.

LAST ROOM? HERE?

RATTLE
WHAT THE HELL? IT'S LOCKED...
RATTLE

!

I THOUGHT SHE SAID IT WAS ON THE RIGHT. COULD SHE HAVE MEANT LEFT?

HOLY MAMA!

AAACK!
INTERESTING NAME. I WAS WONDERING WHY THEY WERE CLEANING THAT OTHER ROOM. ARE YOU THE NEW TENANT?
I'M NOT YOUR MAMA. AND TRUST ME, THERE'S NOTHING HOLY ABOUT ME. WHO ARE YOU?
YES!
Ji-Ae Lee
18 years old
One wild little kitten. Ji-Ae loves to play, and when the game is seducing men, there's none better. She knows no shame, and once she's got a man in her sights, watch out! She, uh, also started school a year late.
DEAR GOD!
YOU'RE SO HANDSOME...
WHAT SORT OF PLACE IS THE OLD MAN RUNNING HERE?!

HEH. I FORGOT TO GIVE HIM THE KEY. HOW SILLY OF ME!
HOMINA HOMINA! WHOA!!
?
WHEN THE OLD MAN TOLD ME TO GO TO BED, I DON'T THINK THIS WAS WHAT HE MEANT!
HOW DID A NICE, BIG BOY LIKE YOU END UP WITH FOOD ALL OVER YOUR FACE? HERE... I'LL LICK IT OFF FOR YOU.
HUH? OH, HI, SEUNG-AH. I WAS JUST SAYING HELLO TO OUR NEW TENANT.
I, UH, DIDN'T REALIZE YOU TWO KNEW EACH OTHER.
WE DON'T! SEUNG-AH! NO! THIS IS NOT WHAT IT LOOKS LIKE!
SEUNG-AH! HELP!
You're such a tease.
CHAMP

GOODNIGHT!
휘익
SEUNG-AH!
팅
SEUNG-AH!
NEWSPAPER!
GOTTA LOVE THIS MORNING AIR. BY THE WAY, SEUNG-AH, DIDJA GET THAT NEW GUY TO HIS ROOM LAST NIGHT?
HUH? OH, UH... YES.
WELL...NOT REALLY.
?
Mine!

MAN, I REALLY SCREWED UP LAST NIGHT. I HOPE SEUNG-AH ISN'T TOO UPSET.
뚜벅 뚜벅
SEUNG-AH?

LIGHTS OUT™

hing
Mine!
Gun
Ji-Ae
Gung-Gun Nam
Gun
Ji-Ae
So cute!
You're mine!
Gun, you're mine starting today.
Gun
Ji-Ae
Seung-Ah
STUDIO GRAFFITY '92
GUESS

The next day...

?

EXCUSE ME, HOW DO I GET TO THE NORTHERN ART SCHOOL FROM HERE?

Best squid in town!

WELL, IF YOU TAKE THE BUS FROM HERE, YOU'LL HAVE TO SWITCH BUSES BEFORE YOU GET THERE. IF YOU TAKE THE SUBWAY, IT'LL TAKE YOU STRAIGHT THERE...

OKAY, THANKS!

7:10 a.m.
I'LL TAKE THE SUBWAY. I REALLY DON'T WANNA SWITCH BUSES!
휙익

UH...OH— YEAH...
YOU KNOW, MAYBE THAT'S NOT SUCH A GOOD IDEA.

YEAH, THE BUS WILL TOTALLY BE BETTER!
휘익
BUT I DON'T HAVE MUCH TIME! THE SUBWAY WOULD BE FASTER. CRAP! I DON'T KNOW WHAT TO DO.
휙
휘익
우물우물
My, my! Time sure does fly. Now it's 8:30, and Gun's late for school.
I CAN'T MAKE UP MY MIND! OH, DAD, WHAT SHOULD I DO?
CK TOCK TICK TOCK TICK TO
TOCK TICK TOCK TICK TOCK
Starting to get mad at himself.
GRAFFITY
LOOK, BUDDY, YOU GONNA GET ON THE BUS OR WHAT?
ACK!!
빙글빙글
휙
우물
쭈물
우왕좌왕
It's 9:00! If it takes you two hours just to decide on a way to get to school, you'll never decide on the best way to apologize to Seung-Ah!
HE REMINDS ME OF MY SON. OH GOD, I HATE MY LIFE...

AT LAST!

I FOUND IT!

SIGN: Northern Art School

One of Northern Art School's gangs

MAN, I'M SO BORED. WHADDYA SAY WE HANG FOR A FEW MORE HOURS? NO ONE'LL MISS US.

I DUNNO WHY EUN-HEE IS SO OBSESSED WITH THAT CHICK. WHY DOESN'T HE JUST TAKE CARE OF IT HIMSELF?

SHUT UP, IDIOT. HE MIGHT HEAR YOU. SHE'S NO ORDINARY CHICK, ANYWAY. SHE RIDES A GIXXER, AND I HEAR SHE HAD QUITE A REPUTATION AT HER PREVIOUS SCHOOL...IF YA KNOW WHAT I MEAN.

EH? HE DOESN'T EVEN HAVE A SCHOOL UNIFORM. IS HE NEW? SURE HOPE SO, MAN. THINGS 'ROUND HERE ARE GETTING SO DULL.
What kinda lameass school is this BIG?! I'm so late I might as well not show up.
Found the school, but has been wandering the campus for an hour trying to find the student admissions office.
HEY, YOU! COME HERE FOR A MINUTE!
HUH?
GRAFFITI
OH, GOOD! THE TWO OF YOU CAN HELP ME FIND THE STUDENT ADMISSIONS OFFICE!
IS THIS KID TELLING US WHAT TO DO?!
YOU'VE GOT SOME NERVE, YA LITTLE PUNK!
DO YOU HAVE ANY IDEA WHO WE ARE?!
HE'S NEW. LET'S TEACH HIM A LESSON ABOUT HOW WE DO THINGS AROUND HERE...
HEY!

WHAT A LOSER. HOLD YOUR HEAD UP, KID. THE REAL LESSON'S ABOUT TO BEGIN.
UNDERCLASSMEN THESE DAYS REALLY HAVE NO MANNERS, DO THEY?
OWW!

쪼르르
I'M... BLEEDING?

뚜둑
AAAGGGGGHHHHH!!
퍽
빡
팍
딱
빡
퍽
우지끈
빡
퍼억
딱
우직
빠억

WHAT A WASTE OF TIME! NOW WHAT DO I DO? IT'S MY FIRST DAY HERE, AND I'VE ALREADY MADE A MESS...
저벅
저벅
Why'd they have to make such a big deal over giving me directions?
OH, WELL... LET'S SEE IF I CAN FIND THE STUPID OFFICE BEFORE IT GETS DARK.

THAT KID'S GONNA GO PLACES...
YEAH, HE'LL FIT IN JUST FINE AROUND HERE.
치이이이이이익
쉬이
쿠
쿵

!

CLASS, THIS IS GUNG-GUN NAM. HE'S OUR NEW TRANSFER STUDENT.

UNTIL HE GETS ADJUSTED TO NORTHERN ART, THERE ARE A LOT OF THINGS HE MAY HAVE TROUBLE WITH...

...SO PLEASE HELP HIM OUT WHENEVER YOU CAN.

HI! NICE TO MEET YOU ALL!

HMM... HE NEEDS A PLACE TO SIT...

톡톡

......
HEY, GEEK! MOVE BACK A SEAT!

Ji-Ae Lee, 18 yrs old, 10th grade, Northern Art School

HMM... I THINK THERE'S AN EMPTY SEAT NEXT TO SEUNG-AH...
SEUNG-AH?!

TEACHER, THERE'S AN EMPTY SEAT RIGHT HERE!!

NOT HER!

OH? WELL, I GUESS YOU CAN SIT NEXT TO JI-AE!
FANCY MEETING YOU HERE...

NOOO!

I'VE GOT A BAD FEELING ABOUT THIS...
THE ONLY GOOD THING THAT CAN COME FROM TWO GIRLS SURE AIN'T GONNA HAPPEN IN A CLASSROOM!

OOH... IT IS JUST ME, OR IS IT HOT IN HERE?

OOOKAY...WELL, THERE GOES THIS UNIFORM. NOTE TO SELF--BUY BIGGER PANTS.

HE'S SO INNOCENT. JUST LIKE A LITTLE BOY...

IT'S SWELTERING IN HERE. I JUST CAN'T STAND IT ANYMORE...

OOPS! THIS DESK IS SO SLIPPERY!!
OH, GOD!
!!
OH, PLEASE NO!
MR. BIG
AAAAH! I CAN'T BELIEVE I JUST DID THAT!

I'LL NEVER BE ABLE TO SHOW MY FACE IN PUBLIC AGAIN!
MR. NAM, I'M NORMALLY ALL FOR EXPRESSING YOURSELF IN CLASS, BUT THIS IS NOT WHAT I MEANT!
TEACHER! HELP ME!
teacher
THWAK!
THAT'S ENOUGH OUT OF YOU! AND I MEAN THAT QUITE LITERALLY!
?!
WHOO! TEACHER SCHOOLED HIS ASS!
Wha...? Why me...?
MANTRA
CLASS DISMISSED!!

I CAN'T KEEP SCREWING UP LIKE THIS, ESPECIALLY NOT IN FRONT OF SEUNG-AH. SHE MUST THINK I'M AN IDIOT!

SEUNG-AH!

......!!!
꾸울꺽
Gulp!

SO, UH, YESTERDAY... YOU KNOW, IN JI-AE'S ROOM? I WASN'T THERE ON PURPOSE. I GOT LOST, AND JI-AE JUST KEPT COMING ON TO ME...AND...

I MEAN... WHAT I'M TRYING TO SAY IS...

SILLY...

SILLY...
SILLY...
SILLY... SILLY!
YOU DON'T NEED TO EXPLAIN YOURSELF, GUN. THERE'S NOTHING BETWEEN US.
울먹
BUT I NEVER EVER WANT TO SEE YOU AGAIN!!
탁탁탁
탁
Gun's family is prone to frequent nosebleeds. It's a genetic thing.
NOSE-BLEEDS ARE SUCH A PAIN. WHY CAN'T MY FAMILY JUST GO BALD LIKE EVERYONE ELSE?!
SEUNG-AH... SHE TOTALLY HATES ME NOW! MAN, I JUST NEED SOME CAFFEINE...
LEMONADE
OPEN 07:00~01:30
AH, MY MISSPENT YOUTH...
Aluminum cans are important resources. Let's all recycle.
나오는
CAFFEINE, YOU'RE THE ONLY ONE WHO CAN FILL MY EMPTY HEART!

Today just isn't his lucky day, is it?
OKAY, NOW I'M *REALLY* PISSED!
I'M SICK OF EVERYTHING MAKING ME LOOK LIKE AN IDIOT!
EVEN THE DAMN SODA MACHINE IS AGAINST ME!
MORON...
The Fuzz

HEY, SEUNG-AH!
NA-RAE?

Na-Rae

WE NEVER SEE EACH OTHER ANYMORE!
OUCH! SORRY, SORRY!

WHERE HAVE YOU BEEN?

DOESN'T MATTER. THE IMPORTANT THING IS THAT I COME BEARING NEWS...

LIGHTS OUT™

BIKE SHOP
행운관
AIR
AIR
Lights Out SD Theater
STUDIO GRAFFITI IN SEOUL
METAL SPIRIT

GUNG-GUN NAM?

YEAH! REMEMBER, I WORK PART-TIME AT MYUNG DONG VILLAGE NOW? THAT'S WHERE I SAW HIM!
STUDIO GRAFFI IN SEOUL
OH...

HE WAS COMPLETELY SURROUNDED BY THIS GIANT GANG OF PICKPOCKETS, AND HE BEAT THEM ALL...WITH JUST ONE FIST!
나불나불
HUH?

BUT Y'KNOW WHAT? I DUNNO WHY, BUT IN THE BEGINNING HE JUST STOOD THERE AND TOOK IT WITHOUT FIGHTING BACK. AND HE PAID FOR ALL THE DAMAGE THE GANG DID.
HE SURE WASN'T WHAT I EXPECTED.
재잘 재잘
OH, REALLY? THAT'S NICE.

YOU'RE NOT IGNORING ME, NOW, ARE YOU...?
OF COURSE NOT!

SO YOU DON'T BELIEVE ME? I'M TELLING THE TRUTH! YOU USED TO GET SO EXCITED ABOUT GUNG-GUN NAM SIGHTINGS! I SWEAR IT WAS REALLY HIM!
IT'S NOT THAT I DON'T BELIEVE YOU... I'VE JUST GOT SOMETHING ELSE ON MY MIND.
WHAT?

SOMETHING ELSE? OR MAYBE...SOMEBODY ELSE?

NO, NO! IT'S NOBODY!

SUUURE, IT IS. DIDN'T YOU SAY YOU WERE GETTING A NEW RESIDENT AT THE HOUSE? I SMELL SOMETHING FISHY HERE...
THERE'S NO SMELL! I TOLD YOU! IT'S NOBODY!

HA HA! WELL, WHY DON'T I COME OVER TOMORROW AND YOU CAN INTRODUCE ME TO MR. NOBODY?
Bye-bye!

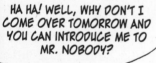

THERE'S NO FOOLING YOU, IS THERE? OKAY, SEE YOU TOMORROW!

MAYBE YOU CAN EXPLAIN THE WAY I'M ACTING TO ME. ALL I KNOW IS THAT EVER SINCE I MET GUN, I HAVEN'T BEEN ABLE TO GET HIM OFF MY MIND.

THE FIRST TIME I SAW HIM, MY HEART WAS BEATING SO FAST... AND THEN, FOR HIM TO BE RENTING A ROOM AT OUR RESIDENCE, OF ALL PLACES...

HUH? WAIT A MINUTE!!

WASN'T GUN'S FULL NAME GUNG-GUN? IT IS! AND HIS LAST NAME'S NAM! OH GOD, I'M SO STUPID!

I DON'T SEE HOW THIS DAY COULD GET ANY WORSE!

SIGN: Lucky Residence

SEUNG-AH THINKS I'M A PERVERT, AND WEIRDASS PICKPOCKETS AND PSYCHO FEMALES KEEP TRYING TO GET BETWEEN US! UGH!

AND I FELT SO GOOD ABOUT MOVING IN HERE! WHAT THE HELL HAPPENED? GOD, I DON'T EVEN KNOW WHAT KIND OF KINKY THINGS JI-AE HAS PLANNED FOR ME WHEN I GET BACK. OH, PLEASE DON'T LET ANYTHING ELSE GO WRONG...

DOOR SIGN: Nam, Gung-Gun

FORGET IT! I'M GONNA TAKE A NAP.

HUH?

OH, I'M SO SORRY! HEH HEH! I GUESS I GOT THE WRONG ROOM AGAIN!
META
WHAT THE HELL'S WRONG WITH ME? MAYBE I SHOULD GET MY HEAD EXAMINED...
SORRY!

HUH?
남궁 전

DOOR SIGN: Nam, Gung-Gun

WAIT, THAT IS MY ROOM!
SO WHO THE HELL IS THAT GUY?!
HEY!
HOW DID YOU GET IN HERE?!
STOP!

WHO ARE YOU?!
GRAFFITY
NGO
THINK YOU CAN ESCAPE THROUGH THE WINDOW? I THINK NOT!
GRAFFITY
NGO
FLYING ATTACK!!!

OH, SHIT.
WHOO! I'M ALIVE!
AAGH..
EEK!
FOOT
DREAM, LOVE AND
STUDIO GRAFFITY
IN
SEOUL
BWAP!!

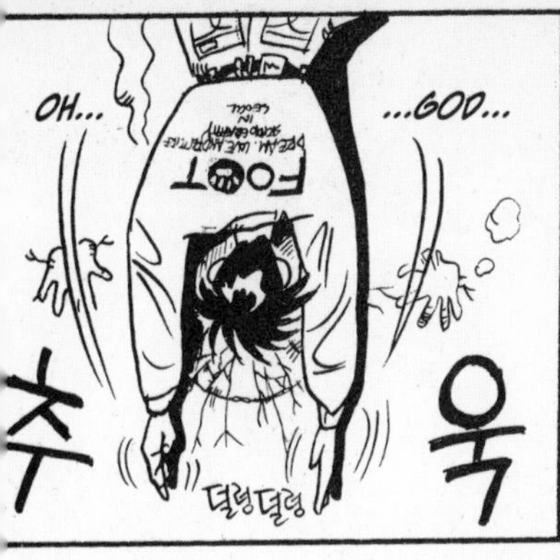
OH...
...GOD...

WHY HAVE YOU FORSAKEN ME?

OWW... NOW, WHERE THE HELL DID THAT WEIRD DUDE DISAPPEAR TO?

COULD HE REALLY BE GUNG-GUN NAM?!

THE GUNG-GUN NAM? FROM JI-JON HIGH SCHOOL?

THAT UNBELIEVABLE STRENGTH... THAT LIGHT IN HIS EYES...

SEUNG-A

HE HAS TO BE! WHAT ARE THE CHANCES OF MEETING SOMEONE WITH THE EXACT SAME NAME?

CREEPY GUYS ARE HANGING OUT IN MY BEDROOM, CRAZY GIRLS ARE COMING ON TO ME LEFT AND RIGHT, AND NOW I'VE GOTTA MAKE DINNER. LOOKS LIKE I'LL BE HAVING RAMEN TONIGHT... AND TOMORROW, AND THE NIGHT AFTER THAT... MAN, I REALLY NEED TO LEARN HOW TO COOK.

YIKES!!

SEUNG...
SEUNG-AH!
th-thump th-thump th-thump th-thump th-thump
th-thump th-thump

Gulp!
꾸울꺽
스윽

I SHOULD JUST ASK HIM. WHY BEAT AROUND THE BUSH? I'LL ASK HIM IF HE'S THE SAME GUNG-GUN NAM.
두근
두근

GUN, CAN I ASK YOU SOMETHING?

ACTUALLY...

BUT HE SEEMS LIKE SUCH A DORK...
Heh heh...
WHAT? WHAT?
Ha!
Ha ha ha!
She's really pretty...
Idiot!

OH? IS THAT ALL...RAMEN?

OH, THIS? YEAH, I'M DEAD BROKE AND I CAN'T COOK, SO THIS IS DINNER...FOR PRETTY MUCH THE REST OF MY LIFE.

I CAN'T BELIEVE THIS GUY...
...IS THE INFAMOUS GUNG-GUN NAM OF JI-JON HIGH. THE NAME MUST BE A COINCIDENCE.

AND...SEUNG-AH, I WANTED TO TALK TO YOU. ABOUT YESTERDAY AND TODAY...
......

SORRY! DON'T KNOW WHAT YOU'RE TALKING ABOUT!
...!!

LIFE IS A LONG, LONELY HIGHWAY.
후루룩
HOW PATHETIC. IF YOU'D TOLD ME A WEEK AGO THAT I'D BE EATING RAMEN AND HAVING GIRL PROBLEMS, I'D HAVE NEVER BELIEVED IT.

LIGHTS OUT™

STUDIO
GRAFFITY
열림

AAACK!!

OH NO!! MY SEXY, ONE-OF-A-KIND RACING JACKET!!

I CAN'T TAKE IT ANYMORE! WHO THE HELL'S MAKING ALL THAT NOISE?!

IS THIS THE ROOM?!

THERE ARE OTHER PEOPLE LIVING HERE, YA JERK! COULD YOU TURN DOWN THE DAMN VOLUME?!

OH, YOU HAVE GOT TO BE KIDDING ME...

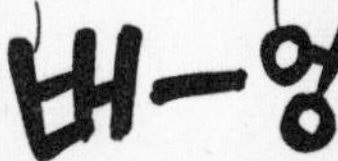

HUH? WAIT A MINUTE! AREN'T YOU THE GUY WHO WAS GOING THROUGH MY STUFF? I *KNEW* YOU LOOKED SUSPICIOUS!!

YO, GUN!

HE KNOWS WHO I AM?

YOU GOT A THING FOR SEUNG-AH, DON'T YA?

METAL SPIRIT

Heh heh

heh heh...

Sung-Rae Roh, 26 years old
Sung-Rae's been living at the Lucky Residence for the last three years--without paying--and has been known to go through other people's stuff without their permission. He has a burning passion for heavy metal.

GREAT, JUST WHAT I NEED. A PSYCHIC PSYCHOTIC.

HOW DO YOU KNOW SO MUCH ABOUT ME?

AH...THAT'S AN EASY ONE, MAN. IT'S WRITTEN ALL OVER YOUR FACE-- ***AND*** IN YOUR JOURNAL.
METALICA

YOU READ MY...?! ***WHO THE HELL ARE YOU AND WHAT WERE YOU DOING IN MY ROOM?!***

RELAX, MAN...

HERE, WHY DON'T YOU HAVE A SEAT, AND I'LL FILL YOU IN...
SPIRIT
EH...

OKAY, THANKS.
스윽
SQUEAK!

HUH? METAL FOLDING CHAIRS AREN'T SUPPOSED TO BE SQUISHY...

A MOUSE?!
쭈우욱

EEEEEEEEEK!
휘리리릭
Heh heh heh...
휘릭

BWA HA HA HA!
YOU'RE THE SEVENTH GUY TO FALL FOR THAT! WHAT A LOSER!
쿵쿵쿵
우하하
Heh heh heh!

EH...?
이글이글
METAL

YOU THINK THAT'S FUNNY, FREAK?!

WE'LL SEE HOW LOUD YOU LAUGH WITH YOUR MOUTH SWOLLEN SHUT!!

DON'T YOU WANNA KNOW HOW TO SCORE SOME POINTS WITH SEUNG-AH?

AAH! HEY, NO, WAIT!

SEUNG-AH?!
GO ON! TELL ME!
I'M ALL EARS!
......!!
솔깃~
하늘하늘
띵
솔깃

WELL,
IT'S A LONG,
COMPLICATED
STORY...
METAL SPIRIT

NO PROBLEM!
CAN I GET YOU
ANYTHING?
SODA? JUICE?
BACKRUB?
AAH,
THAT'S GOOD.
A LITTLE
LOWER...

SO, LAST NIGHT, YOU WENT
INTO JI-AE'S ROOM
ON ACCIDENT AND
WERE CAUGHT
BY SEUNG-AH,
RIGHT?
HUH? OH, HI, SEUNG-AH. I WAS JUST SAYING HELLO TO OUR NEW TENANT.
NO!
!!!
NO! I...

HE KNOWS ABOUT THAT, TOO?
HOW MUCH DOES THIS GUY KNOW...?

HA HA... THAT'S NOTHING. I KNOW *EVERYTHING* THAT'S GOING ON UNDER THIS ROOF. NOTHING ESCAPES MY WATCHFUL EYE!
SPIRIT

USING THE LATEST STATE OF THE ART TECHNOLOGY...

...SOMETIMES AS A HOBBY...

...SOMETIMES FOR SURVIVAL...
That free-loader said he was gonna pay the rent today!

...I'M ABLE TO KEEP CLOSE TABS ON ALL OF THE LUCKY RESIDENTS! I KNOW EVERYTHING ABOUT EVERYONE! AND, GUN, WITH A LITTLE BIT OF ASS-KISSING ON YOUR PART, I'LL TELL YOU HOW THE ANGELIC SEUNG-AH CAN BE YOURS!

HMM...
HE SEEMS SINCERE, BUT IS HE?
FINE! TELL ME!
TELL ME HOW TO WIN SEUNG-AH'S HEART!
HEH! THAT'S EASY...
ALL YOU GOTTA DO...

...IS BE A COOL PERVERT LIKE ME!
METAL SPIRIT
HUH? HUH? WHATCHA THINK? AREN'T I SEXY? C'MON, EVEN *YOU* WOULD FALL FOR THIS!
Like a graceful ballerina...~♪
TH-TH-THAT....

THAT IS THE STUPIDEST THING I'VE EVER HEARD!!!
TAKE THIS! DRAGON SUPLEX!!

DO I LOOK LIKE AN IDIOT?!

ERR... OOPS! WELL, SO MUCH FOR CONTROLLING MY TEMPER...

HEH. SORRY... SOMETIMES I GET MAD, AND...
Oww...

DO YOU EVEN REALIZE WHY SEUNG-AH RAN OUTTA THERE LAST NIGHT?
METAL SPIRIT
SHE'S A WOMAN, MAN!

THAT'S RIGHT! SHE IS! SO WHAT YOU'RE SAYING IS THAT SEUNG-AH MIGHT LIKE ME, TOO?
WOW! NOTHIN' GETS BY YOU, DOES IT?

SO SHE WAS THINKING ABOUT ME, TOO!
YEAH, SO WHAT ***YOU*** GOTTA DO IS BE A MAN AND LET HER KNOW ***SHE'S*** YOUR WOMAN.
METAL SPI

HEY, SUNG-RAE, YOU'RE ALL RIGHT! THANKS!
NO SWEAT. IF YOU HAVE ANY PROBLEMS, JUST COME SEE ME.
METAL SPIRIT

SCHWEET!!!
HE'S SUCH A NICE YOUNG MAN... WE'LL SEE HOW LONG THAT LASTS.

MILK

STUDIO GRAFF IN SEOUL

DINGLE

쪼르르르...

OH! IT'S ALREADY TEN!

AAAH...

YEAH, I'M DEAD BROKE AND I CAN'T COOK, SO THIS IS DINNER...
OH, GUN...

CRRIK CRRIK
HE MUST BE STARVING FOR SOME REAL FOOD AFTER EATING NOTHING BUT RAMEN. I'LL TAKE HIM SOME CAKE AND MILK.

I'LL APOLOGIZE FOR RUNNING OFF ON HIM TODAY, TOO. THAT'LL SURPRISE HIM. I SURE HOPE HE'S NOT ALREADY ASLEEP...

보글
보글
보글
DAMN, NO MATTER HOW MUCH I EAT, I'M STILL HUNGRY.
Om nom nom...

LET'S SEE IF I CAN SCORE SOMETHING OTHER THAN RAMEN!
FLICK

GUN! I MADE A CAKE, AND I WAS WONDERING IF YOU'D LIKE A PIECE!
남궁 건
똑
똑
똑

CAN I COME IN?

LIGHTS OUT™

......??

딸칵

HUH...? HE'S NOT HERE.
벌컹~

THAT'S STRANGE... MAYBE HE'S IN THE BATHROOM.
차륵
I'LL JUST WAIT FOR HIM.

THIS ROOM... IT BRINGS BACK SO MANY MEMORIES OF MY MOM.

IF ONLY SHE COULD SEE HER ROOM NOW...

두근 두근
OR SEE WHAT HAPPENED TO ME YESTERDAY ON THE SUBWAY...

AAH! WHAT AM I THINKING?!

WHAT'S THE MATTER WITH ME? I'M ACTING LIKE A STUPID SCHOOLGIRL!

LOOKS LIKE THE COAST IS CLEAR!

A REFRIGERATOR! OH, HOW I LOVE YOUR HEAVENLY HUM...

HEH HEH HEH... AT LAST! REAL FOOD!
HA HA HA!

부들
부들

I SHOULDN'T BE DOING THIS...

...BUT AFTER THREE DAYS OF STARVING TO DEATH, I JUST CAN'T HELP IT.
Agh agh...

HEH HEH... HA HA... BWA HA HA HAAA!!!

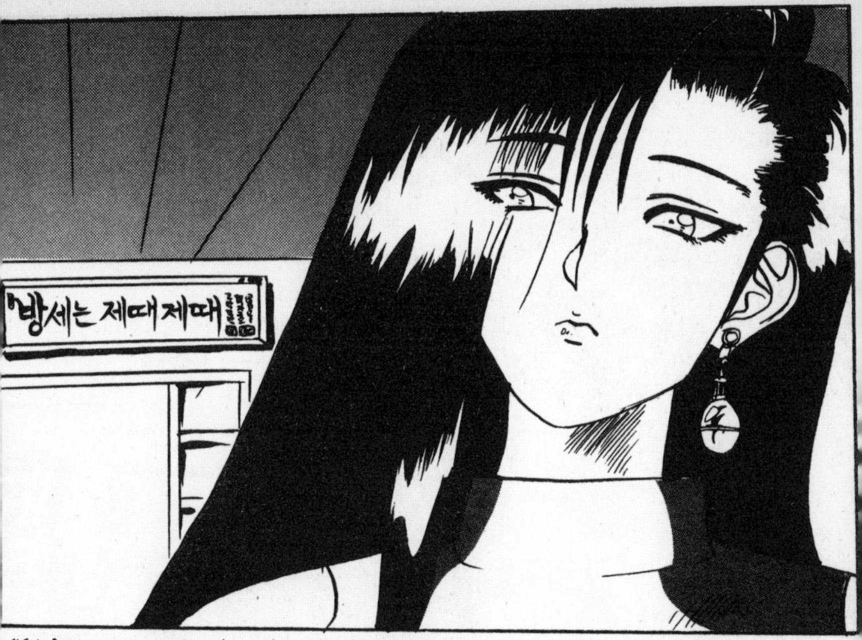

방세는 제때제때

SIGN: Rent money must be paid on time. NO EXCEPTIONS!!

WHAT I WOULDN'T GIVE FOR A GOOD, GENUINE MAN TO SINK MY TEETH INTO. I'M SO BORED WITH ALL THESE BOYS.
THEY'RE ALL SO CHILDISH AND IMMATURE... HMPH!

JUST HOW LONG MUST I WAIT FOR MY PRINCE CHARMING?
HUH?

MILK
EH?!

OH NO! JI-AE!
I'M DOOMED!

SPEAKING OF SINKING YOUR TEETH INTO SOMETHING...

HI, JI-AE! WHAT BRINGS YOU DOWN HERE?
NEVER THOUGHT I'D FIND *YOU* IN A KITCHEN!
FREE-SPIRITED GIRL LIKE YOURSELF...

SILLY GUN! IF YOU WERE HUNGRY, YOU SHOULD HAVE COME AND SEEN ME. I CAN SATISFY THE MOST INSATIABLE OF... APPETITES.
스윽

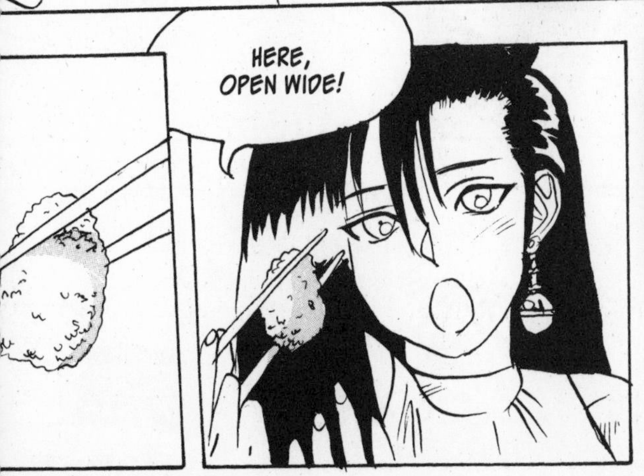
HERE, OPEN WIDE!

oooooo !!

WOW, IT SURE TASTES BETTER WHEN *YOU* GIVE IT TO ME!
REALLY?

YOU LOOK SO CUTE WHEN YOU'RE EATING, GUN!
와작

SHE SEEMS DIFFERENT THAN WHEN WE WERE IN SCHOOL TODAY. SHE'S ACTING DOWNRIGHT GENTLE.

IT'S ALREADY 11 O'CLOCK. WHERE COULD HE BE?

OH, WELL. I'LL JUST HAVE TO LEAVE IT HERE.

HERE COMES THE AIRPLANE!
AAAAH!

OOPSIE!
미끄

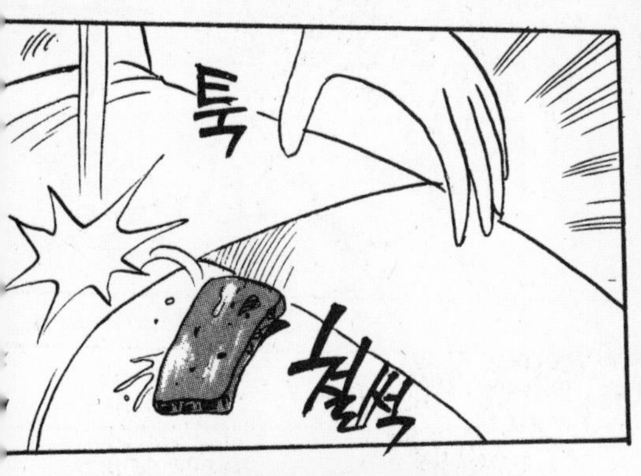
툭

UH?!
삐질

OH DEAR, WHAT TO DO? IT'D BE SUCH A WASTE TO THROW IT AWAY...
쪼르르...

HERE, EAT THIS.
WHY DO I HAVE A BAD FEELING ABOUT THIS?

↑ Ji-Ae's fingers

OH, GUN!
HOW CAN I MAKE YOU LOVE ME?

Gun's having trouble swallowing.
OF COURSE NOT!
우물우물
Gulp!
꿀꺽

GUN? ARE YOU OKAY? YOU'RE NOT CHOKING, ARE YOU?

HI, GUN! I'M A TALKING SHRIMP! DON'T YOU WANT TO EAT ME?!

YOUR OWN FINGERS? REALLY?
WELL... YEAH.

OKAY, THE TALKING SHRIMP THING IS A LITTLE WEIRD. YOU KNOW, MAYBE IT'S BEST IF I JUST EAT THEM WITH MY OWN FINGERS.

OKAY!

OH, MAN! I THINK I MAY HAVE STEPPED IN IT AGAIN...

OH NO! THE CHOPSTICKS!

SHE DID THAT ON PURPOSE!

YOU'RE A MAN, AREN'T YOU? WELL, A REAL MAN DOESN'T GO BACK ON HIS WORD, GUN!
Hey!
SO USE YOUR DAM FINGERS.
AH! AAH! AAAH!!!
WELL, THAT WAS A BLOODY WASTE OF TIME...
?!!

Gun's dazed and confused.

My prince!♥

S-SEUNG-AH?! I SWEAR THIS ISN'T WHAT IT LOOKS LIKE! I DIDN'T STEAL FOOD FROM THE FRIDGE OR DO ANYTHING KINKY WITH JI-AE!

WHAM!!

SEUNG-AH, WAIT!
YOU DON'T UNDERSTAND!!

STAR LIGHT, STAR BRIGHT. SUNG-RAE SAID I WAS A LOSER, AND, MAN, WAS HE RIGHT!

I CAN'T BELIEVE THAT PUNKASS 10TH GRADER DID THIS TO US!
NEITHER CAN I, BUT SHUT UP. IF EUN-HEE SEES US, WE'RE...
The next day.

UGH!

JUNG-DAE? SUK-PYO? YOU GUYS LOOK UGLIER THAN USUAL. WHAT THE HELL HAPPENED TO YOU TWO?

B-BOSS!!

LIGHTS OUT™

I ♥ GUN
Cafe

UN-FREAKIN'-BELIEVABLE.

Eun-Hee Kang
19 years old
The best fighter at Northern Art High School. Known for his amazing strength, Eun-Hee's special move is the "human bomb," a technique that can be used only by a man of his stature. He hates his girly name, but he loves Seung-Ah.

AGH! EUN-HEE!

HEEGK!

I THOUGHT I TOLD YOU NEVER TO USE MY REAL NAME!!

AGGCK!!

IDIOT.

JUNG-DAE!

YES, BOSS?

TELL ME WHAT HAPPENED. DID SOMEBODY BEAT YOU GUYS UP?

UHH...SUK-PYO AND I WERE RIDING A MOTORCYCLE AND CRASHED...
덜덜덜

찌릿
REALLY?

OF COURSE! DO YOU THINK I COULD EVER LIE TO YOU, EUN-HEE?

EUN-HEE!

DIDN'T WE JUST GO THROUGH THIS?! SOMEONE ATE THEIR ***STUPID FLAKES*** THIS MORNING!

NOOO! I'M SORRY! ***PLEASE, NOT THAT!***

YAAH!

TAKE THIS!
HUMAN BOMB!
AAAAAAH!!
HA
HAVE A NICE NAP, YOU LOSERS.
꿈틀 꿈틀
꿈틀
I BID MUH TOND.

딩동
CLASS DISMISSED!
딩동 딩동

YOU STILL GOT THAT BLIND DATE SET UP FOR TONIGHT?
YEAH, MAN! GOT A COUPLE OF HOT ONES!
와글 와글
우르르
BYE, CHUN-JA! SEE YOU TOMORROW!
OH YEAH!

UH...SEUNG-AH, HI!

......!

OH MAN! SHE'S STILL MAD AT ME ABOUT LAST NIGHT!

Na-Rae Shin
17 years old
Na-Rae is Seung-Ah's friend. She knows more about the boys at other high schools than anyone else. In short, she's Northern Art High School's walking, talking little black book.

STREET FIGHTER II
CAPCOM®

HMM... SHOULD I AGREE TO GO OUT WITH THOSE BOYS FROM JOONG-ANG HIGH TOMORROW?
TEL

THIS SEUNG-GOO GUY LOOKS PRETTY CUTE...

MAYBE I'LL CALL HIM... HUH?

GUNG-GUN NAM!

WHAT'S HE DOING WITH ALL THAT LUGGAGE?

IT'S BEEN TWO HOURS ALREADY. ARE YOU SURE YOU KNOW WHERE WE'RE GOING?

OF COURSE, SONNY. JUST LEAVE THOSE HERE.
SURE.

THANK YOU, YOUNG MAN! YOU DESERVE SOME TEA OR COOKIES! I DON'T SEE TOO MANY GOOD KIDS LIKE YOU THESE DAYS! BLESS YOU!
OH NO, I'M JUST GLAD I COULD HELP!
UGH, MY ARMS ARE KILLING ME. STILL, IT FEELS GOOD TO DO SOMETHING NICE.
Ha ha! Sucker!
Bye-bye!

HUH?

HI, GUN!

I'M SORRY... DO I KNOW YOU?

THAT'S COLD! I STILL REMEMBER *YOU.*

OH YEAH! I ASKED YOU ABOUT THE OWNER OF THE SHOP THAT I WRECKED AT MYUNG DONG VILLAGE!
NOW YOU REMEMBER? GOD, YOU'RE DENSE...

He did well to remember at all!

JUNG-DAE, AIN'T THAT HIM?
......
.....!
...?..
......!!
THAT'S HIM.

PUNKASS 10TH GRADER, PICKING UP CHICKS WHILE WE LOOK LIKE THIS? YEAH, LAUGH IT UP, BUDDY. IT WILL BE YOUR LAST.

IF EUN-HEE FINDS OUT THAT KID BEAT US UP, HE'LL SKIN US ALIVE. WE NEED TO TAKE CARE OF HIM WITHOUT ANYBODY KNOWING. WAIT, ISN'T THAT GIRL...?

HE'S TALKING TO NA-RAE SHIN, NORTHERN ART SCHOOL'S BEST SOURCE OF STUDENT INFORMATION! EXCELLENT. WE'LL USE HER TO GET TO HIM!

TAKE CARE!
HERE'S OUR CHANCE!

SO I WAS RIGHT.

'SCUSE ME. I'M AFRAID YOU'LL HAVE TO COME WITH US.

HUH?

McDUNALD

WHAT KINDA CRAZY CHICK EATS THIS MUCH? THAT'S HER SEVENTH BURGER!
SHIT, MAN! I CAN'T EVEN AFFORD A FRENCH FRY WITH WHAT SHE LEFT ME.

ALL RIGHT, IT'S TIME FOR YOU TO STOP STUFFING YOUR FACE AND TELL US SOMETHING! WHO WAS THAT GUY THAT YOU WERE TALKING WITH AFTER SCHOOL?!
GUY?

OH, HIM! NO WONDER YOU GUYS SEEM SO EXCITED!

HE'S THE LEGENDARY GUNG-GUN NAM FROM JI-JON HIGH. HE TRANSFERRED TO OUR SCHOOL YESTERDAY. YOU GUYS MUST'VE HEARD.
오물
오물

WHAT?! GUNG-GUN NAM?! AT OUR SCHOOL?!

HE'S THE DUDE THAT'S BEEN KNOCKING AROUND ALL THE GANGS, INCLUDING THE ONES FROM JI-JON. HE'S FAMOUS, EVEN AROUND HERE... HE'S THAT GUNG-GUN NAM?!

WHY DOESN'T ANYBODY BELIEVE ME? I'M TELLING THE TRUTH. TWO DAYS AGO, HE TOOK DOWN A GUY TWICE HIS SIZE WITH ONE PUNCH! I WAS THERE! I SAW IT!
NO WAY... HE CAN'T BE THE SAME GUY.
Nah...

WHAT?! BUT THAT WOULD MAKE HIM NEARLY EUN-HEE'S SIZE! OH MAN, IT ALL MAKES SENSE NOW. NO WONDER HE LAID US OUT SO EASILY!
IT MIGHT BE A DIRTY WAY TO FIGHT, BUT WE CAN'T TAKE ANY CHANCES.
THIS IS SERIOUS!
Northern Art Gangs 10th and 11th grades
HEY, NUMBERS DON'T GUARANTEE WE'LL WIN. THIS GUY AIN'T HUMAN!
YEAH!
HUH?
?
LET'S GET THE GUYS! WE'RE GONNA NEED BACKUP!

HERE HE COMES!

HEY, YOU! THAT'S RIGHT! I'M TALKING TO YOU! ***GUN NAM!***

YEAH, WE'VE HEARD OF YOU. WE'VE GOT US A LITTLE SOMETHING TO TALK ABOUT.

AH, CRAP.

LIGHTS OUT™

WHO ARE YOU GUYS?
TRUST ME. YOU'RE GOING TO GET TO KNOW US VERY WELL, GUN.
GREEEAT. THEY KNOW WHO I AM. I PROBABLY SHOULDN'T HAVE MESSED WITH THEM YESTERDAY.
I DUNNO WHO THIS GUN GUY IS YOU KEEP TALKING ABOUT. IF I RUN INTO HIM, I'LL TELL HIM YOU'RE LOOKING FOR HIM. NOW, IF THERE'S NOTHING ELSE, I GOTTA GET GOING. BYE!
YOU'RE NOT GOING ANYWHERE, PAL.

I DON'T KNOW HOW YOU DID THINGS AT JI-JON, BUT YOU'RE AT NORTHERN ART NOW, AND WE DO THINGS DIFFERENTLY HERE. DO WE UNDERSTAND EACH OTHER, GUNG-GUN NAM?
OH NO, I'M NOT *THAT* GUNG-GUN NAM.
YOU'RE NOT?
WELL THEN, GET LOST, YOU FAKE!
HEY! WHO THREW THAT SHOE?! WE DIDN'T TELL ANYONE TO START THROWIN' SHOES! DAMMIT!!
Huh?
AAAAH!

HIS PUNK ASS IS MINE!

THIS GUY'S GONNA KILL US. WHO'S IDEA WAS IT TO ROUND UP ALL THE GANGS AGAIN?
OH, MAN... OUR BRILLIANT PLAN IS FALLING APART. FIRST SOME GUY THROWS A SHOE, NOW BORIS HERE WANTS TO KILL HIM. THIS IS ALL GOING DOWNHILL FAST.

!

AAAGH!!

HGGGH!

UNREAL... THIS LITTLE GUY'S A COMPLETE BADASS!

AH, HELL. WE CAN'T HIDE NOW. WHATEVER HAPPENS, HAPPENS!

THERE'S NO TURNING BACK! WE'LL FIGHT HIM TOGETHER! WE'LL KICK HIS ASS TOGETHER!
EXCEPT FOR THE GUY WHO THREW THE SHOE. YOU CAN'T KICK ANYONE'S ASS BAREFOOT, YOU IDIOT.

THE REST OF YOU, TEAR THIS JERK TO PIECES!!!

HYAAAH!

URRGH!
Oh, man! He's the real deal.

WAAH?!
HE'S TOO STRONG!!

QUICK!

AND!

FAST!

DELI-
VERY!

이리 상회
TEL. 464-X896
신속배달

Sung-Rae Roh
26 years old
Remember him? He's the perverted metalhead from Lucky Residence! Right now he's working as a part-time deliveryman at a local rice store (yet he still has absolutely no intention of paying rent).

HEEE!

RRGH!
다다다

HUH?
SPIRIT
파파파

SCREEEEEEECH!!!

THAT GUY LOOKS FAMILIAR...
Sung-Rae's shoe!

WAIT, ISN'T THAT GUN?
~휘윳♪
Damn!

EUN-HEE!
BOOF!

SIGN: Lucky Residence

RICE!

RICE!

RICE!

RICE!

METAL SPIRIT

YO! SEUNG-AH!
HOW'S IT GOIN'?

OH, SUNG-RAE!
HI! ARE YOU
WORKING?

METAL

YEAH, AND BY THE WAY...
YOU KNOW THAT NEW GUY,
GUNG-GUN NAM?

WHAT
ABOUT HIM?

SPIRIT
OH, NOTHIN' BIG. HE'S JUST FIGHTING YOUR SCHOOL GANG AROUND THE CORNER THERE...

OKAY, GOTTA GO. BYE!

MY SCHOOL GANG? DOES HE MEAN EUN-HEE'S BOYS?
GUN...?

WHAT ARE YOU DOING? HAVE YOU ALREADY FORGOTTEN YOUR PROMISE?

YOUR PROMISE TO YOUR MOTHER--IT WAS YOUR WHOLE REASON FOR TRANSFERRING OUT HERE, AFTER ALL.

Huff! Huff! Huff! Huff! Huff! Huff! Huff!

OK

Head throbbing...

HELLUVA WAY TO MAKE AN ENTRANCE.

LIGHTS OUT™

I ADMIRE YOUR SKILL, BUT I'M A BIT TOUGHER THAN THESE KIDS. YOUR BIGGEST PROBLEM IS WHETHER YOU'VE STILL GOT THE ENERGY LEFT TO TAKE ME ON.

WELL, ISN'T THIS INTERESTING? YOU'VE BEATEN FIFTY OF MY TOUGHEST, MOST LOYAL GUYS... I'M NOT EVEN SURE I COULD DO THAT.

HUFF!

WANNA FIND OUT?

HUFF!

IT'S TIME YOU LEARN YOUR PLACE!
THE GAME ENDS NOW! EVEN IF I DON'T FIGHT YOU MYSELF, YOU'LL NEVER STAND A CHANCE AGAINST HYUN-SUK AND DAE-SUNG!
Heh.
THE THREE POLAR STARS!!
THEN HE MUST BE...
Three Polar Stars Eun-Hee Kang, Hyun-Suk Yang and Dae-Sung Suh Even without Eun-Hee, their power of destruction is unfathomable. The three are idolized by all Northern High gangs.
Huff!
NO, GUN! YOU'LL NEVER BEAT EUN-HEE! EVEN IF YOU ARE WHO I THINK YOU ARE!
Huff!
SKWORSH!
Huff!

WHAT'S WRONG, GUNNY-BOY?! YOU SCARED? YOU GONNA CRY? *HA HA HA!!*

EUN-HEE, EH? THAT'S AN AWFULLY GIRLY NAME. TELL ME, WAS YOUR MOM EXPECTING A GIRL? YOU SURE RUN YOUR MOUTH LIKE ONE.

Hurk!

Egak!

SO YOU THINK MY NAME IS GIRLY, DO YA? YOU THINK I RUN MY MOUTH? WELL, LET'S SEE HOW A PUNK LIKE YOU FARES AGAINST A GIRLY LITTLE MAN LIKE ME, SHALL WE?

OH, SHIT! HYUN-SUK, HE'S GOT THAT LOOK IN HIS EYES AGAIN.
EUN-HEE, CALM DOWN! IT'S US, MAN!

LET'S SEE HOW YOU FARE AGAINST MY HUMAN BOMB!
OH, CRAP!
FINAL FANTASTIC SPECIAL ULTRA GREAT ATOMIC THUNDERBOLT HYPER ORIGINAL BUBBLE BLAST BOMBER!

GUN, I GOT A NOTE FROM THE SCHOOL TODAY. THEY SAY YOU WERE IN ANOTHER FIGHT. OH, GUN. WHEN ARE YOU GOING TO STOP THIS?
RIGHT BACK ATCHA!
Su-Ji Nam
36 years old
Gun's mother. Watch this space for details!
AAAGH!

I PROMISE, MOM. I PROMISE THAT NO MATTER WHAT HAPPENS, I'LL NEVER FIGHT AGAIN I'LL TRANSFER TO A DIFFERENT SCHOOL AND LIVE THE LIFE YOU WANT ME TO!

HUFF!

HUFF!

I HAD A TALK WITH YOUR TEACHER. SHE TOLD ME THAT YOU WERE EXPELLED, AND THAT THERE WAS NOTHING SHE COULD DO. HOW AM I GOING TO FACE YOUR FATHER WHEN I SEE HIM IN HEAVEN?

Is she his mom or sister?!

OOPS!

Yaaah!

BWAAK!!

CHEW ON THAT, PUNK!

RRRGH!

YOU MESSED WITH THE WRONG GUY!

Ngh!

YOU'RE THE ONE WHO MESSED WITH THE WRONG GUY, EUN-HEE!

NO, GUN! THINK OF ME! THINK OF YOUR POOR, DEAD FATHER!
RGH!

DON'T CAUSE ANY TROUBLE AT YOUR NEW SCHOOL, GUN! PLEASE? FOR ME? FOR YOUR DEAD DAD?
두근 두근
OH, MOM!
AN OPENING!
빡
WHAM!!!

AGH!

YOU'RE FINISHED, PUNK!! YOU'RE YESTERDAY'S NEWS!!

foot!!!

SO THIS IS THE MIGHTY GUNG-GUN NAM. I HEARD YOU WERE A KILLER, BUT YOU'RE JUST A SNIVELING LITTLE BOY. PATHETIC.

Huff!
Huff!
Huff!

G-G-G...

HA HA HA!

GUN!! GET UP! DON'T JUST LIE THERE AND BLEED! FIGHT BACK!!

SEUNG-AH!!
WHAT'S THIS?!

LIGHTS OUT™

WHAT THE...?! THAT LITTLE BRAT!
SEE, LOOK AT THAT! COMPARED TO OUR ONE AND ONLY EUN-HEE, EVEN GUN NAM AIN'T NOTHIN' BUT A--
WAIT, LOOK!
AFTER ALL THAT, HE CAN STILL GET UP?!
STAY DOWN, YOU JERK!
ARRGHH!!

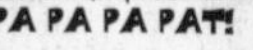
PA PA PA PAT!

GUN!!

....!!
EEEK!

FAST!
AND!
QUICK!
DELI-VERY!
IT'S OUR TURN!! LET'S SHOW 'EM WHAT WE'RE MADE OF!!
WOOT!!
BOSS! YOU ARE DA MAN, MAN! LOOK, LET US SOFTEN HIM UP FOR YA. LEAST WE CAN DO. GIVE HIM A FEW BRUISES ACROSS THE OL' BACKSIDE, YA DIG?
WHY AM I REMINDED OF GULLIVER'S TRAVELS ALL OF A SUDDEN?
N-NOT THE OL' BACK-SIDE...
....

HRRRRGGGH!
UH... OKAY. THAT WASN'T SUPPOSED TO HAPPEN.
IS THAT THE BEST YOU PUNKS CAN DO?!
EEEEK!

DON'T UNDERESTIMATE THE POLAR STARS, YOU LITTLE WORM!
HUNH?!
TAKE THIS! BISON SHOULDER THROW!!

ERGH... YOU LITTLE...
HOW DARE YOU?!

OH, NO HE DIDN'T!

YOU STAY RIGHT THERE, SON! DADDY'S GOT SOME TENDER, LOVING CARE FOR YOU!!
BWAK!

NO WAY! HE GOT THE BOSS, MAN! WE'RE DEAD!
WELL, LET'S NOT JUMP TO CONCLUSIONS HERE. THE BOSS *LETS* HIMSELF GET JACKED UP EVERY NOW AND THEN.
HE LIKES IT BETTER WHEN PEOPLE THINK HE ALMOST GOT HIS ASS KICKED. LIKE HE'S RALLIED BACK FROM BEHIND OR SOMETHING. THE CHICKS LOVE IT.
HA HA HA! WELL, ALL RIGHT, KID! THIS IS GETTING INTERESTING!

SOON'S YOU LET ME GO, YOU'RE...
덜렁
덜렁

...THE NEW BOSS!

ARE YOU FREAKIN' KIDDING ME?!

SEUNG-AH, I REALLY DIDN'T WANT YOU TO SEE THIS SIDE OF ME.

TH-THUMP!
TH-THUMP!

YOU LOSERS!! WHO CARES IF I WAS HOT SHIT AT JI-JON OR NOT?! JUST LEAVE ME THE HELL ALONE!!
척
휙

I DON'T WANT TO SEE YOUR UGLY ASSES AGAIN.

IT REALLY IS HIM!!

OH, GUN... I-I THINK I MIGHT UNDERSTAND A LITTLE BIT ABOUT HOW YOU FEEL...

HEY, BOSS!
YOU ALIVE?

HA! HE'S COMPLETELY DOWN FOR THE COUNT! SOME BOSS! HE DIDN'T DO ANY BETTER THAN THE REST OF US!!
Everyone secretly hates their boss.

IT'S A NEW DAY, GENTLEMEN! EUN-HEE'S REGIME IS AT AN END!
HA HA HA HA HA HA!

HEY, YOU!! EUN-HEE!!
HEY, EUN-HEE! EUN-HEE!
EUN-HEE! EUN-HEE! EUN-HEE!!

And that day, the cries of the 10th and 11th graders could be heard for miles away...

SAY IT LOUDER, MEN! HA HA! OH MAN, THERE'S NOTHIN' FUNNIER THAN ENDLESSLY REPEATING THIS GUY'S NAME!

HEY, EUNNY!! PAGING EUN...
TH-THUMP TH-THUMP

번쩍

-HEE!!!
OH, CRAP.

SORRY! I'M SORRY! NO, PLEASE! I DIDN'T MEAN IT! THESE GUYS MADE ME DO IT!!!

I STILL GOT ENOUGH STRENGTH TO BUST YOUR SORRY ASS! ***HUMAN BOMB!!***

SCREAM OUT MY NAME, HUH? HOW ABOUT YOU SCREAM IN PAIN INSTEAD?!

THWOK!!

PFFT!
WHO'S NEXT?!
Aiiee!
GOD, TESTOSTERONE IS SO PATHETIC WHEN LEFT UNCHECKED.

LIGHTS OUT™

HEY, SWEET THING! Y'DON'T HAFTA BUY IT, BUT TAKE A LOOK AT THE NEW WALKMAN I GOT HERE. I GOT A LOTTA NEW MERCHANDISE!!
Calvin Klein
CAN YOU SHOW ME THAT?
!
I CAN SHOW YOU ANYTHING YOU WANT, BABY.
TOK TOK
MIC
PONE

WAIA
AREA 88
89.1
Y'KNOW, IT'S THE LATEST IN TECHNOLOGY!

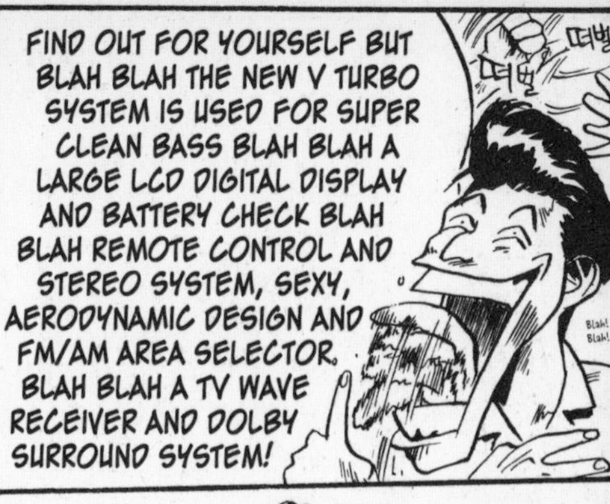
FIND OUT FOR YOURSELF BUT BLAH BLAH THE NEW V TURBO SYSTEM IS USED FOR SUPER CLEAN BASS BLAH BLAH A LARGE LCD DIGITAL DISPLAY AND BATTERY CHECK BLAH BLAH REMOTE CONTROL AND STEREO SYSTEM, SEXY, AERODYNAMIC DESIGN AND FM/AM AREA SELECTOR. BLAH BLAH A TV WAVE RECEIVER AND DOLBY SURROUND SYSTEM!
떠벌
떠벌
Blah! Blah!

Yeah! That's right! That's how you should do business!

DOUBLE HEAD AND AUTO TAPE SELECTOR, AND HUNDREDS OF OTHER HIGH TECH AND ***EXPENSIVE*** FEATURES! HUH?

SO HOW MUCH IS IT?

HOW MUCH IS IT? I DON'T HAVE ALL DAY...

YOU HAVE ***SUCH*** GOOD TASTE. IT'S NOT CHEAP, BUT WHAT YOU'RE GETTING IS TOP OF THE LINE!

HUH? WHAT THE--?! THAT WOMAN'S SELLING FISH TOPLESS!

WHERE?

NO, SHE'S NOT.

BUT, WHAT'S THAT GOT TO DO WITH... HUH?!
SHE STOLE IT!
THIEF!!!
DAMN, HE'S NOISY...
Mina Kim
17 years old
Northern Art School's most delinquent girl, Mina looks at the world through a very twisted perspective and has a knack for burglary. She's rough around the edges, but she really just needs some love... Oh, and she just got out of a juvenile detention center today.

HUH?
YEAH, I'D BETTER EAT FIRST.
MINI MART
HELLO!
SECURITY'S NOT TOO TIGHT...
HYAAAARGH!
No clue.

HEH HEH...
MY MASTERPIECE.
GREATEST.
WORK. EVER.
SMIRK

NOW I JUST GOTTA GET OUTTA HERE...

WHAT KINDA MINI MART HAS ABSOLUTELY NOTHING TO BUY?!
WELL, WHAT WERE YOU LOOKING FOR?

당탕!
주렁주렁
UH, NOTHING. I WAS HUNGRY, BUT NOW, ALL OF A SUDDEN, I'M STUFFED.

STUFFED?! YOU'RE SO CLEVER! PLEASE MOP CAREFULLY!
DAMN.
GRAFFITI

The next morning...
YO! GOOD MORNING!

GUYS...

...AND GALS, ALL LOOKING FRESH AND ENERGETIC!!

WHAT?!

IS TODAY THE DAY WE'RE SUPPOSED TO START WEARING OUR SUMMER UNIFORMS?

GUY'S CRAZY.
GUESS HE COULDN'T AFFORD THE SUMMER UNIFOR
WHAT'S UP WITH THAT GUY?!
HEAT EXHAUSTION, DUDE. HE'S STILL WEARING HIS WINTER UNIFORM.

GUN...
EEK!
IT'S ALL GOOD! A HOT GUY LIKE ME IS ALWAYS IN STYLE!
I GUESS YOU DIDN'T HEAR THAT WE WERE SUPPOSED TO SWITCH TO SUMMER UNIFORMS TODAY.
Urk!
AAAAH! I HATE SUMMER!!

Gun's trademark pose!!

Gym

GOOD! FIRST ONE TO RUN TEN LAPS CAN GO BACK TO THE CLASSROOM AND KICK BACK FOR THE REST OF THE PERIOD!

YEAH!!

HEH HEH!

Eh?
Huh?

COMIN' THROUGH!!

Is he nuts?!

RRRRRRRRGH!

You! Pace yourself! Slow down!
10th lap
Huff!
Huff!
Huff!
2nd lap
2nd lap
3rd lap
1st lap

ONE MINUTE 59 SECONDS!! I CAN'T BELIEVE IT! IN ALL MY YEARS AS AN INSTRUCTOR, I'VE NEVER SEEN SUCH SPEED!

THE NEW TRANSFER STUDENT... GUNG-GUN NAM, WAS IT?! THIS GUY'S GONNA WIN SOME GOLD MEDALS FOR SURE!
HEY, TEACHER! LOOKS LIKE I'M FIRST! HEH...
Get him to the ER!

HEH, IT'S BEEN A FEW MONTHS, BUT THIS OLD DUMP HASN'T CHANGED AT ALL.

It's her first day back, so she's wearing the winter uniform.

1 – 7

OF COURSE, THERE ARE USUALLY ***STUDENTS*** IN ALL THESE SEATS.

WHERE IS EVERYBODY? IS IT P.E. TIME?

EH, WHATEVER. I'M TAKING A NAP.

NOTE: The sheet of paper Mina's looking at is a tuition stub, meaning that the cash with it is some poor Joe's tuition.

1-

Huff!
Huff!

MAN, I FEEL GREAT! THIS TOTALLY MAKES UP FOR THIS MORNING!

싱글
벙글

Gun!
HEH HEH! EVEN SEUNG-AH GOT TO SEE HOW SEXY I LOOK!

I FEEL LIKE *TODAY* MAY BE THE DAY THAT SOMETHING WONDERFUL HAPPENS TO ME.
AND SO...

HUH?
WOOHOO!

OH NO! NO!!

WHAT'S UP, SUNG-HO?

I KNOW I LEFT IT IN MY PANTS POCKET!

YOUR TUITION'S GONE?!

YEAH! I LOOKED EVERYWHERE. I *KNOW* I HAD IT BEFORE GYM!

WELL, THEN SOMEONE MUST'VE TAKEN IT *DURING* GYM.

HUH?

LIGHTS OUT™

WANTED!!
SEUNG-A, MIN
LET'S GET COOL SUMMER IN NEXT CHAPTER
SUMMER IN STUDIO GRAFFITI

WHAT?!

FAR AS I CAN TELL, WE'RE LOOKING AT ONE OF TWO SCENARIOS HERE. SCENARIO ONE: SUNG-HO'S TUITION MONEY JUMPS OUT OF HIS POCKET AND RUNS AWAY. OR SCENARIO TWO: THE NEW GUY STOLE IT WHILE HE WAS HANGING OUT IN THE CLASSROOM. WHICH ONE SOUNDS MORE LIKELY?

THE FIRST ONE.

ALL HELL'S PROBABLY BREAKING LOOSE IN CLASS BY NOW...BUT HEY, NOT MY PROBLEM!
WHAT?! SOMEBODY LOST SOME MONEY?! OH NO!
Ack! Mina!
Ow!

YEAH, IT WAS THIS GUY!

!

Gun

UGH!

HEY! HE'S THAT GUY WHO KICKED EUN-HEE'S SORRY ASS YESTERDAY! GUN NAM, OR SOMETHING LIKE THAT. TOUGH BREAK. HE'S KINDA CUTE.

Croak.

Other students as seen by Mina

CRAP. HE'S GETTING HEAT FROM THE ENTIRE CLASS. WHAT A BUNCH OF WHINY ASSHOLES.
GIVE IT BACK!
I SENSE AN OPPORTUNITY HERE.
I CAN'T LET A FELLOW BADASS TAKE THE HEAT. AND I'VE BEEN LOOKING TO STICK IT TO THIS LITTLE SHIT FOR MONTHS NOW.
!

A NICE LITTLE FUNDS TRANSFER. I SHOULD WORK AT A BANK.
반짝
반짝
Clueless
Cock-a-doo!
WHAT? WHOSE TUITION'S MISSING?
MINA! YOU'RE JUST IN TIME! THIS GUY SWIPED SOME MONEY, AND NOW HE'S ACTING LIKE HE DOESN'T KNOW ANYTHING ABOUT IT. SINCE YOU'RE AN EXPERT ON STEALING STUFF, MAYBE YOU COULD...
NICE TO SEE MY REPUTATION PRECEDES ME. LITTLE PUNK'S GONNA PAY FOR THAT COMMENT.
EH?
두리번
EH?
?
두리번
WHAT ARE YOU LOOKIN' AT?! THIS IS THE GUY RIGHT HERE!
HUH?
Hgk!
DING DING DING!! WE HAVE A WINNER!
HEEEEEGH!

HA! SO YOU THOUGHT YOU WERE GONNA STEAL IT AND BLAME IT ALL ON HIM, HUH? DUMBASS!
WHAT?
But how?
Why?
YOU RAT BASTARD!! WHY DONCHA TAKE *THIS* INSTEAD?!
URRRGH!
퍽
퍽
퍽
Heh!
BUT...IT WASN'T HIM!
Bastard!!
?

CLASS DISMISSED!

THAT GIRL HAD THE MONEY. SHE WAS THE REAL THIEF!

HUH?

YOU WANT WE SHOULD CARRY YOUR BOOKS FOR YOU? HUH, BOSS?
......

GET OUTTA MY WAY!
디——잉!
So humble! Carrying his own books...

HUH?

HA HA HA!

Hee

Clueless

THAT POOR BASTARD DOESN'T EVEN REALIZE HE'S JUST BEEN ROBBED.

HEY, WAKE UP!

짝

짝 짝 짝

SO DO YA WANNA BE OUR BOSS NOW?

NO! DO YOU KNOW THAT GIRL OVER THERE?

I'm pretty, oh so pretty...
...!
YEAH, THAT'S YOUR MOM!
HRK!
THWAK

HER NAME'S MINA, DUDE. SHE'S BEEN IN A DETENTION CENTER SINCE EARLIER THIS SEMESTER FOR STEALING CRAP. THE CRAZY THING IS THAT I THINK HER FAMILY'S RICH. SHE STEALS TO GET HER KICKS. KNOW WHAT I MEAN? SHE'S BAD NEWS, MAN. EVEN THE GANG GUYS STAY AWAY. IF SHE'S BACK HERE, ALL I CAN SAY IS KEEP AN EYE ON YOUR WALLET.
MINA, HUH?

GO BUY YOURSELF SOME FOOD WITH THIS!
OH?

HANG IN THERE, KID! WORK HARD AND DON'T GROW UP TO BE A BEGGAR, ALL RIGHT?

THANKS!

......!!

I DON'T GET IT. SHE'S GOT A HEART OF GOLD...SO WHY...?

두리번
두리번
EXCUSE ME!

I BELIEVE THAT COSTS 2000 WON.
HEY! GET YOUR HANDS OFF ME, YOU CREEP!
GUN!

WHOA! YOU'VE GOT SOME STRONG HANDS.
YOU DON'T HAVE TO DO THIS, YOU KNOW. THE STEALING? IT'S BENEATH YOU.
HE... HE'S SO HOT!! BUT...
화끈...
TH-THUMP
TH-THUMP
TH-THUMP
!!
BENEATH ME? LIKE YOU'D KNOW!
RRRRGH!
덜덜덜덜
찌—잉...
STOP ACTING LIKE YOU KNOW ME, YA SEXIST JERK!

!

자연세제

……!

WELL,
WHAT DO YOU KNOW?
LOOKS LIKE MR. KNOW-
IT-ALL'S OPINION MAY
ACTUALLY MATTER
TO ME.

LIGHTS OUT™

GRAFFITI!!

YAAAAH!
MAN, I'M BEIN' ROASTED ALIVE HERE! HOW CAN ANYONE SURVIVE IN HEAT LIKE THIS? WHAT'S WITH THIS PLACE? THEY CAN'T AFFORD AIR CONDITIONING? YEESH. NO WONDER RENT'S SO CHEAP!
AT LEAST THE WATER HERE IS COLD...
AAAH... THE ICE JUST MELTS IN MY...

YAAAAAAAHHH!!
THERE'S A FREAKING EYEBALL IN MY WATER!!
AAAIIIIEEEE!!!
GUUUUN... GIVE ME BACK MY EYEBALL, GUN!
HUH?!
Gun doesn't like horror movies!

IT'S GONNA GET ME FROM BEHIND!
DUDE, DO YOU HAVE ANY IDEA HOW DIRTY THAT SOUNDS?

I AM *NOT* IN THE MOOD, MAN!
SPIRIT
Urrrggh...

OWW... AND HERE I WAS GONNA TELL YOU A SPECIAL SECRET, JUST FOR YOU, 'CUZ WE GET ALONG SO WELL, AND 'CUZ I THOUGHT WE WERE BUDS...

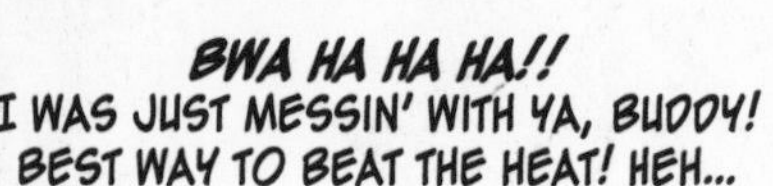
BWA HA HA HA!!
I WAS JUST MESSIN' WITH YA, BUDDY!
BEST WAY TO BEAT THE HEAT! HEH...

IT WAS YOU?
TAL SPIRIT

SECRET? IS IT SEUNG-AH'S MEASUREMENTS?!
YOU PERVERT. NAH, ACTUALLY, I WANTED TO TELL YOU ABOUT...
...THE GHOSTS OF LUCKY RESIDENCE!
GHOSTS OF LUCKY RESIDENCE?!
두근
YOU SEE, THERE'S THIS INTERESTING...PHENOMENON THAT ONLY HAPPENS IN THE SUMMER, ON HOT RAINY NIGHTS AND ONLY TO THE NEWEST RESIDENT OF THE HOUSE. I'M NOT SURE IF YOU KNEW THIS, BUT THE LUCKY RESIDENCE USED TO BE A HOSPITAL IN THE KOREAN WAR, SO IT ONLY MAKES SENSE THAT THERE'D BE GHOSTS HERE. ALL THE DEAD SOLDIERS AND ALL.
AH, MAN... HOW DID HE KNOW THAT GHOST STORIES REALLY FREAK ME OUT?
SPECIAL WIND

IT'S ONLY A STORY! YOU CAN'T LET IT GET TO YOU. NOT UNLESS YOU WANT TO LOSE ALL CREDIBILITY AS A MAN.
THAT'S RIGHT. I'M A **MAN,** DAMMIT! AND MEN AREN'T AFRAID OF ANYTHING!
MOMMY?
WHAT AM I DOING?! THERE'S NOTHING TO BE AFRAID OF! IT'S JUST A THUNDERSTORM! AND THE BEST THING TO DO IN A THUNDERSTORM IS TO CLOSE THE CURTAINS AND GO TO BED EARLY! YEP!
EH?

WHAT'S THAT?

WOO!

WOO!

SOMETIMES THE HEADLESS GHOSTS OUTSIDE TRY TO GET INTO THE HOUSE AND TAKE THE HEAD OF THE NEWEST RESIDENT. SO I'M WARNING YOU, NO MATTER WHAT HAPPENS, DON'T LEAVE YOUR ROOM!!

HEADLESS GHOSTS! THERE ARE HEADLESS GHOSTS RIGHT OUTSIDE MY WINDOW!!!

METAL SPIRIT

"ONLY A TEN PERCENT CHANCE OF RAIN" MY ASS!

I GOTTA GET OUTTA HERE!

MIST IN THE HALLWAY! OH, GOD! THERE'S MIST IN THE HALLWAY!!!
STUDIO GRAFFITI
AND THEN, THE HALLS FILL WITH A MYSTERIOUS MIST!

A HOT, STEAMY BATH IS THE BEST THING FOR A HOT, STEAMY NIGHT! OOPS, DID I FORGET TO CLOSE THE BATHROOM DOOR AGAIN?

SHHHH

AND THEN... FOOTSTEPS!
CREEEEK TAT CREEEEK TAT
TAT TAT TAT TAT

OH, MAN! MY HEAD IS POUNDING! I'M GONNA GET SOME ICE WATER FROM DOWNSTAIRS...

AND WHEN THE FOOTSTEPS STOP, THAT'S WHEN THE GHOST GIRL APPEARS...WITH A HEAD ON A PLATTER!

GetALife
STUDIO GRAFFITI

JUST THE SOUL I WAS LOOKING FOR! CARE FOR A BITE? IT'S VERY SWEET....

?
AAAAH!
THE SCARY GHOST
LADY IS GONNA GET ME!

DON'T LOOK BACK! JUST RUN FOR ALL YOU'RE WORTH! OH, GOD! SHE WAS TERRIFYING!!

꿈틀
꿈틀
HUH? WHAT'S THAT UP AHEAD? IS IT A MOUSE?

스믈
스믈
WHAT?!

NOOOOO!!
AND IN THE HALLWAY, A SEVERED HAND ROAMS, SEARCHING FOR THE WOUNDED SOLDIER TO WHOM IT BELONGS!
노성래
DON'T HURT ME, PLEEEEASE!!!
WHAM!!!
휘적
휘적
WHERE'S MY BLASTED SCREWDRIVER?
He's under the floor fixing the circuits.
Remember him? It's Seung-Ah's grandpa!

UGH... OH, MAN. MY HEAD HURTS LIKE HELL. WHERE AM I?
HEY, GUN! WE'RE FRIENDS, RIGHT? YOU AND I?
WELL, THEN I HOPE YOU DON'T TAKE THIS THE WRONG WAY OR ANYTHING, BUT I'VE JUST GOTTA KNOW. CALL IT A MORBID CURIOSITY OR SOMETHING. ALL I KNOW IS IF YOU DON'T TELL ME, I'M GONNA BE WONDERING ABOUT IT EVERY DAY FOR THE REST OF MY LIFE. TELL ME, DUDE...
...DID YOU PISS YOUR PANTS?
METAL SPIR
Heh heh heh...
I MEAN, THE LOOK ON YOUR FACE...
YOU PSYCHOTIC ASS! C'MERE SO I CAN DROPKICK YOU!
YEAH, THAT'S GONNA HAPPEN!
SLOW DOWN, YOU FAST AND QUICK FREAK!
HA HA HA!!
Ah, poor Gun... Three beautiful women are clamoring for him, and the only action he's found at the Lucky Residence is from a slightly psychotic metalhead. Lights out! We'll see you in Volume 2!

In the next volume of

LIGHTS OUT™

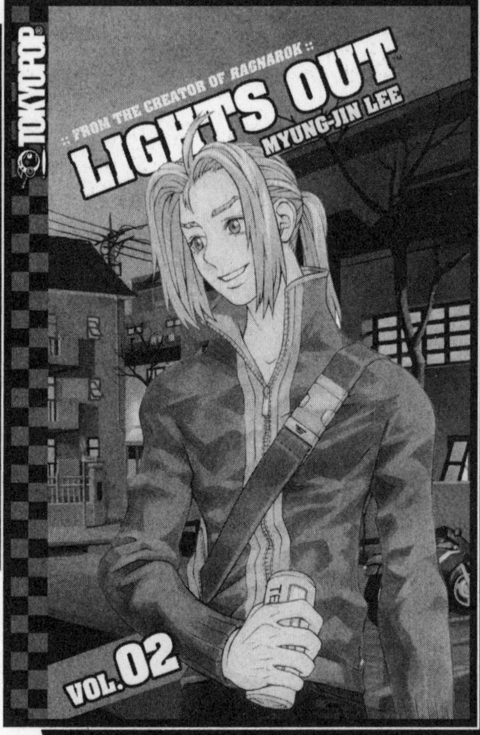
TOKYOPOP
:: FROM THE CREATOR OF RAGNAROK ::
LIGHTS OUT™
MYUNG-JIN LEE
VOL. 02

Already having a difficult time adjusting to life at a new home and school, things only get worse for Gun with the sudden appearance of Seung-Hyuk, a famous motorcyclist and close friend of Seung-Ah. A former tenant of the Lucky Residence, everyone seems to love Seung-Hyuk...everyone except Gun, that is. Determined to beat this new threat at his own game, Gun enters the Grand Prix, a famous Korean motorcycle race. If Gun has the chops to defeat the dynamic Seung-Hyuk, Seung-Ah will be his! Of course, maybe he should actually learn how to race first...

TAKUHAI 宅配
WANNA DO TAKUHAI?
THE NEW SIZZLING HOT MANGA MAGAZINE
SIGN UP FOR FREE
www.TOKYOPOP.com
Princess Ai © & TM TOKYOPOP Inc. and Kitty Radio, Inc.

Ai from *Princess Ai*

DRAMACON™

Sometimes even two's a crowd.

When Christie settles in the Artist Alley of her first-ever anime convention, she only sees it as an opportunity to promote the comic she has started with her boyfriend. But conventions are never what you expect, and soon a whirlwind of events sweeps Christie off her feet and changes her life. Who is the mysterious cosplayer that won't even take off his sunglasses indoors? What do you do when you fall in love with a guy who is going to be miles away from you in just a couple of days?

Svetlana Chmakova's
DRAMACON
TOKYOPOP
V.I.P.
BUMP

CREATED BY SVETLANA CHMAKOVA, CREATOR OF MANGA-STYLE ONLINE COMICS "CHASING RAINBOWS" AND "NIGHT SILVER"!

Preview the manga at:
www.TOKYOPOP.com/dramacon

NO
LOITERING
T
TEEN
AGE 13+

kare kano
MASAMI TSUDA

BY MASAMI TSUDA

KARE KANO

Kare Kano has a fan following for a reason: believable, well-developed characters. Of course, the art is phenomenal, ranging from sugary sweet to lightning-bolt powerful. But above all, Masami Tsuda's refreshing concept—a high school king and queen decide once and for all to be honest with each other (and more importantly, themselves)—succeeds because Tsuda-sensei allows us to know her characters as well as she does. Far from being your typical high school shojo, *Kare Kano* delves deep into the psychology of what would normally just be protagonists, antagonists and supporting cast to create a satisfying journey that is far more than the sum of its parts.

~Carol Fox, Editor

BY SHIZURU SEINO

GIRL GOT GAME

There's a fair amount of cross-dressing shojo sports manga out there (no, really), but *Girl Got Game* really sets itself apart by having an unusually charming and very funny story. The art style is light and fun, and Kyo spazzing out always cracks me up. The author throws in a lot of great plot twists, and the great side characters help to make the story just that much more special. Sadly, we're coming up on the final volume, but I give this series credit for not letting the romance drag out unnecessarily or endlessly revisiting the same dilemmas. I'm really looking forward to seeing how the series wraps up!

~Lillian M. Diaz-Przybyl, Jr. Editor

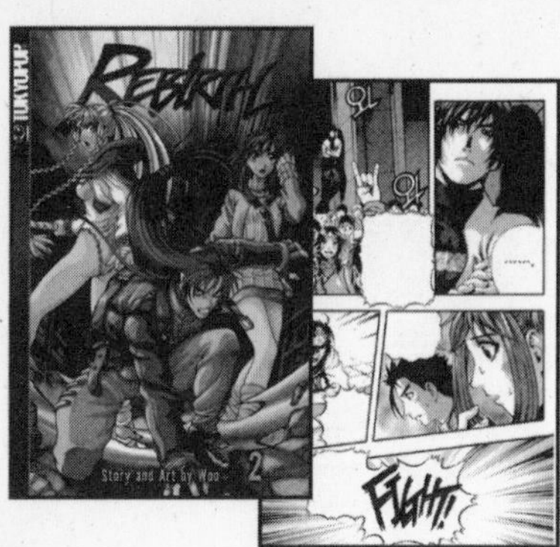
REBIRTH
TOKYOPOP
Story and Art by Woo
2
FIGHT!

BY WOO

REBIRTH

Every manga fan has their "first love." For me, that book is *Rebirth*. I've worked on this series in one fashion or another since its debut, and this epic, action-packed vampire tale has never yet let me down. *Rebirth* is a book that defies expectations as well as first impressions. Yes, it's got the dark, brooding vampire antihero. And, sure, there's lots of bloodshed and tight-bodied maidens in peril. But creator Woo has interwoven an enthralling tale of revenge and redemption that, at its heart, is a truly heartbreaking tragedy. Were you a fan of TV's *Angel*? Do you read Anne Rice? Well, my friend, *Rebirth* is for you!

~Bryce P. Coleman, Editor

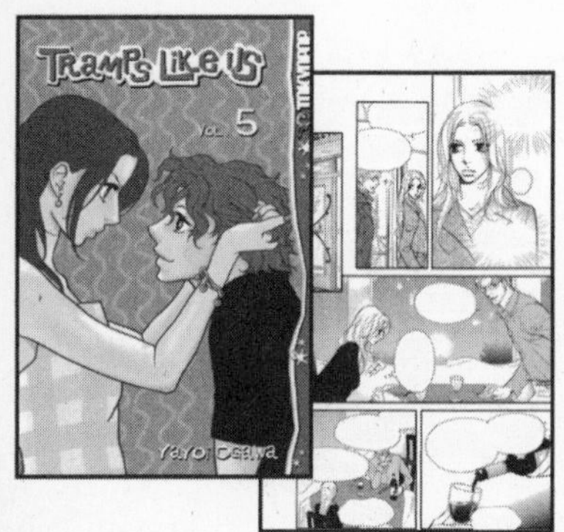
Tramps Like Us
Vol. 5
TOKYOPOP
Yayoi Ogawa

BY YAYOI OGAWA

TRAMPS LIKE US

Thrillingly erotic but relentlessly realistic, *Tramps Like Us* turns gender stereotypes on their head. Sumire Iwaya, a beautiful and busy news exec, is disappointed by the men in her life. So she takes in a gorgeous young boy and makes him her pet. As a man, am I offended? Not really. Actually, I find it really sweet. Sumire is no wide-eyed, skirted, young manga vixen. She's tall, womanly, with a wide mouth and serious, appraising eyes. Momo is cute as a puppy one minute, graceful and petite the next. But the book only indulges the fantasy aspect partway. The abnormal situation gets awkward and even burdensome. I love it. And the tone Carol Fox sets in the English adaptation is one of the best around.

~Luis Reyes, Editor

SPOTLIGHT TOKYOPOP MANGA SUPPLEMENT

SAMURAI CHAMPLOO

BY MASARU GOTSUBO AND MANGLOBE

ANCIENT JAPAN IS ABOUT TO GET A LETHAL DOSE OF STREET JUSTICE–
CHAMPLOO STYLE!
SAMURAI CHAMPLOO
TOKYOPOP
1
Masaru Gotsubo
Manglobe
BASED ON THE POPULAR ANIME SERIES THAT *ANIME INSIDER* CALLS "THE SPIRITUAL SEQUEL TO *COWBOY BEBOP*"!
T
TEEN
AGE 13+
Mugen is a rough-around-the-edges mercenary. Jin is a disciplined samurai. Fuu is a young waitress. These three unlikely companions are about to begin a dangerous quest for a mysterious samurai that will get our heroes into and out of trouble more times than they can count (which admittedly isn't very high).
© Masaru GOTSUBO 2004. © manglobe/Shimoigusa Champloos.

FOR MORE INFORMATION VISIT: WWW.TOKYOPOP.COM